FoR

day.

DON'T VOTE —
It Only Encourages Them!

David Barber

Compiled by
David Barber

Cartoons by
Bob Brockie

£2

ART

24/40

CAPE CATLEY LTD

It doesn't matter who you vote for --
you'll still get a politician

DON'T VOTE - IT ONLY ENCOURAGES THEM

If voting made any difference they'd make it illegal

DEDICATION

This book is dedicated to all political journalists around the world who strive daily to report the truth.

First published November 2004
Cape Catley Ltd
P O Box 32-622
Devonport
North Shore City
New Zealand

Email: cape.catley@xtra.co.nz
Visit our website: www.capecatleybooks.co.nz

Typeset in Carmina Medium 10/13
Designed and typeset by Kate Greenaway, North Shore City
Cover cartoon: Bob Brockie, Wellington
Cover design: Mix CVS Ltd, North Shore City
Printed by Publishing Press, North Shore City

ISBN: 0-908561-97-0

"In the end, you know, if you were serious in this job you'd go mad," said David Lange, former New Zealand Prime Minister and king of the one-liner, depicted by Brockie having fun while his much more serious deputy Geoffrey Palmer looks on.

CONTENTS

Introduction

After half a century of newspaper work, reporting from a similar number of countries and covering elections on the ground in at least seven of them, I have sadly concluded that most politicians lose their sense of humour overnight upon election. Cheery candidates who have smiled throughout even the roughest campaigns awake as parliamentarians-designate devoid of ability to laugh at themselves.

Hanging onto power is a deadly serious business. Poking even mild fun produces a wan smile at best. Step up the humour and the grin becomes grim, stick in the knife as a brilliant cartoonist like Bob Brockie does weekly and the funny bone is anaesthetised.

Aggrieved, they do not seem to understand that if our elected representatives do not invite us to laugh with them, they cannot be surprised if we laugh at them.

There are exceptions, of course. Former New Zealand Prime Minister David Lange, who provided the best show in town in the 1980s with weekly press conferences peppered with a string of hilarious one-liners, could not help himself. "In the end, you know, if you were serious in this job you'd go mad," he told me at the time.

Lange was an exception, for sadly wit is not a notable feature of modern politics. Elections are now largely fought on television, and the hustings, which once crackled with good-natured verbal thrust and parry, have become dry and humourless. Political correctness rules in an increasingly sensitive society, and minders and spin doctors advise their charges that it is best to be serious. Humour, especially on controversial subjects, is unlikely to give them a boost in the polls, they are told.

Heckling, which traditionally spiced election meetings with wit and laughter, has come to be regarded as akin to sports field hooliganism — at best frowned upon, at worst deplored and liable to provoke aggressive attention from watchdog heavies.

Humour, it seems, has become a political no-no. There are no votes in it. "Never make people laugh," a long-forgotten American senator once advised his president. "If you would succeed in life, you must be solemn, solemn as an ass."

Well, 'ass' may be a word that comes to mind to anyone who observes the proceedings of Parliament.

Actual *debate* is rare as MPs bray at each other across the chamber and attempts at humour tend to be more malicious than witty.

Humans, unlike the ass and other animals, are blessed with a sense of humour and the ability to laugh — at themselves and at each other. History has shown us that democracy is fragile and the wit of politicians flourishes in a democratic society. For the ordinary man and woman, there are few laughs under a dictatorship.

I found the title of this book daubed on a wall in London in 1974, a year Britons were forced to undergo two general elections — an experience to test the most fervent defender of democracy.

Although the humourless will no doubt dub it "irresponsible", it should not be taken too seriously. I have invariably exercised my democratic rights at the ballot box and in 1966 even voted in two countries' general elections on the same day. (Based in Sydney, I had absentee rights as a New Zealand poll voter and voting is compulsory for Australian residents.)

But I have always retained my sense of humour. Unable to come to an honest decision in the campaign for one New Zealand election but determined to vote anyway, I cast my ballot for the now sadly extinct McGillicuddy Serious Party who seemed to me perfect representatives of the political comically absurd.

My partner Ruth, misjudging my love of the ludicrous, refused to believe this until Monday's newspaper breakdown of voting at every polling station showed just one elector had given that party a tick at the booth at the bottom of our street.

Bob Brockie has demonstrated weekly in *The National Business Review* over three decades that he is a brilliant cartoonist and one of the most astute observers of international and domestic politics. I was delighted that he agreed to add his sense of the ridiculous and collaborate on this irreverent look at political life and I acknowledge his contributions with gratitude.

David Barber, Wellington

Authority

"We are ruled by children ... the very instinct of authority is an instinct of immaturity, well worth the pleasure of laughing at, whenever practicable, just to cut it down to size."
Jan Morris, Welsh writer (1926-)

"All authority is quite degrading. It degrades those who exercise it, and it exercises those over whom it is exercised."
Oscar Wilde, Irish playwright and wit (1854-1900)

"Every great advance in natural knowledge has involved the absolute rejection of authority."
T J Huxley, English biologist (1825-95)

Democracy...

An early 20th century French writer, Robert de Flers, described it as: "The name we give to the people each time we need them."

To Sir Winston Churchill, (1874-1965) British wartime leader, it was:
"The worst form of government, except for all those other forms that have been tried from time to time."

While H L Mencken, American commentator and curmudgeon (1880-1956), defined it as:
"The theory that the common people know what they want and deserve to get it good and hard."

Mencken also wrote:
"Under democracy one party always devotes its energies to trying to prove that the other party is unfit to rule – and both commonly succeed and are right."

In other writings the prolific Mencken described democracy as:
"... only a dream; it should be put in the same category as Arcadia, Santa Claus and Heaven."

... and ... "the art and science of running the circus from the monkey cage".

"No word in the vocabulary has been so debased and abused as democracy."
Lord Hartley Shawcross, British lawyer and Labour politician (1902-2003)

"Democracy means government by discussion, but that is only effective if you can stop people talking."
Clement Atlee, British Labour PM (1945-51)

"Democracy is simply the bludgeoning of the people, by the people, for the people."
Oscar Wilde

"Two cheers for democracy - one because it admits variety and two because it permits criticism. Two cheers are quite enough; there is no occasion to give three."
E M Forster, English novelist (1879-1970)

"One must remember that democracy in New Zealand is not a positive thing; it's by regulation, not by right ... In this reach-me-down, ready-made, handed-out, so-called democracy, nothing is right unless it's under clause C, sub-section D of some mouse-trap scrivener's misuse of English."
Denis Glover, New Zealand poet (1912-80)

"Democracy substitutes election by the incompetent many for appointment by the corrupt few."
George Bernard Shaw, Irish playwright (1856-1950)
Man and Superman

Democracy can be fragile, as was demonstrated in the US presidential election that brought George W Bush to power.
As Sir Tom Stoppard, British playwright (1937-) observed in *Jumpers*:
"It's not the voting that's democracy; it's the counting."

And Earl Long, notoriously corrupt Governor of Louisiana (1895-1960) once said:
"The voting machines won't hold me up. If I have the right commissioners, I can make those machines play 'Home Sweet Home'."

So What Exactly is Politics?

"Politics is the conduct of public affairs for private advantage" according to Ambrose Bierce, US journalist (1842-1914) in *The Devil's Dictionary*, while Britain's Dr Samuel Johnson (1709-84) dubbed it: "Nothing more than a means of rising in the world."

Larry Hardiman, an American comic writer, put it this way:
"The word 'politics' is derived from the word 'poly", meaning many, and the word 'ticks', meaning blood-sucking parasites."

"Politics is the diversion of trivial men who, when they succeed at it, become important in the eyes of more trivial men."
George Jean Nathan, US critic-writer (1882-1958)

"Politics and the fate of mankind are shaped by men without ideals and without greatness. Men who have greatness within them don't concern themselves with politics."
Albert Camus, French writer (1913-60)

"The standard of intellect in politics is so low that men of moderate mental capacity have to stoop in order to reach it."
Hilaire Belloc, British writer and one-time MP (1870-1953)

"Being an MP is not really a job for grown-ups – you are wandering around looking for and making trouble."
Ken Livingstone, British Labour politician and Mayor of London

Or in a comment variously attributed to Groucho Marx (1895-1977) and British publisher Sir Ernest Benn (1875-1954):
"Politics is the art of looking for trouble, finding it everywhere, diagnosing it incorrectly and applying the wrong remedies."

"The art of politics consists in knowing precisely when it is necessary to hit an opponent slightly below the belt."
Konrad Adenauer, Chancellor of Germany (1876-1967)

An opportunity to ride the Gravy Train to The Promised Land, according to Brockie, reflecting Dr Johnson's definition of politics as "Nothing more than a means of rising in the world.".

"Politics is a flesh-eating business. It's a blood sport. As soon as you show you've been hurt then everyone's into you."
Mike Moore, briefly Prime Minister of New Zealand 1990 and international diplomat, who also confessed...
"I like my politics as I like my steak - raw and bloody. But there is a limit."

... and Winston Churchill, who knew something about political and military battles, said: "Politics is almost as exciting as war, and quite as dangerous. In war, you can only be killed once, but in politics many times."

"Being in politics is like being a football coach. You have to be smart enough to understand the game and stupid enough to think it's important."
Eugene McCarthy, US politician who unsuccessfully challenged sitting Democratic President Lyndon Johnson in 1968 and ended up writing children's stories.

"Politics is not the art of the possible. It consists of choosing between the disastrous and the unpalatable."
John Kenneth Galbraith (1908-), US economist and diplomat

"Politics I supposed to be the second-oldest profession. I have come to realise that it bears a very close resemblance to the first."
Ronald Reagan, as Governor of California before becoming US President 1981-89

He later conceded:
"Politics is not a bad profession. If you succeed, there are many rewards, and if you disgrace yourself you can always write a book."

... while a predecessor (1961-63) from a very wealthy family, John F. Kennedy, said: "The political world is stimulating. It's the most interesting thing you can do. It beats following the dollar."

"Don't tell my mother I'm in politics – she thinks I play the piano in a whorehouse."
Anonymous US saying from the Depression

... and Harry S Truman (US President 1945-53) confessed later:
"My choice early in life was either to be a piano-player in a whorehouse or a politician. And to tell the truth, there's hardly any difference."

"Just come, without any commitments, and see what happens. Our domestic arrangements are as elastic as the conscience of a politician."
A R D Fairburn, New Zealand poet (in letter to fellow poet Denis Glover)

... who also wrote:
"Oh, what a tangled web we weave
when first we practise to deceive!
And when the practice is perfected
we're just the boys to get elected."

But some politicians resent such cynicism, ex-US president Richard Nixon, for instance, who said in 1973, the year before he resigned under the threat of impeachment over Watergate:
"I reject the cynical view that politics is inevitably, or even usually, a dirty business."

Nixon also said: "When the President does it, that means it is not illegal"... and
"Watergate was worse than a crime — it was a blunder."

"Politics is too serious a matter to be left to the politicians."
Charles de Gaulle, French general and president (1890-1970)

... but Lord Hailsham, British Conservative MP politician (1907-2001) said:
"Politics should be fun. Politicians have no right to be dull or po-faced. The moment politics becomes dull, democracy is in danger."

Hailsham put his philosophy into practice, admitting after he became Lord Chancellor:
"When I'm sitting on the Woolsack in the House of Lords I amuse myself by saying 'Bollocks' sotto voce to the bishops."

"Politicians are the same everywhere. They promise to build a bridge even when there's no river."
Nikita Khrushchev, USSR Premier (1894-1971)

Why Go Into Politics?

It's easy enough, as Scottish writer Robert Louis Stevenson (1850-94) noted in *Familiar Studies of Men and Books*:
"Politics is perhaps the only profession for which no preparation is thought necessary."

Benjamin Disraeli, British statesman (1804-81), who twice became Prime Minister, admitted:
"I love fame; I love public reputation; I love to live in the eyes of the country."

"The only jobs to have in politics are prime minister or minister of finance. All the rest are just branch managers."
Phil Holloway, diplomat and New Zealand Labour MP (1954-60)

Politicians ... So What Are They Really Like?

"The ex-banker has all the necessary attributes of a politician – blinding ambition and complete disregard for loyalty."
John Armstrong, New Zealand journalist on National Party leader Don Brash in the *New Zealand Herald* 2004

"Politicians are like babies' nappies. They should be changed often — for the same reason." Anonymous.

"A good politician is quite as unthinkable as an honest burglar." H L Mencken

While W B Pitkin, an American writer of the 1920s, described them as:
"... the semi-failures in business and the professions, men of mediocre mentality, dubious morality and magnificent commonplaceness."

"My deepest feeling about politicians is that they are dangerous lunatics to be avoided when possible and carefully humoured; people above all to whom one must never tell the truth."
W H Auden, English-born US poet (1907-73)

Politics has often been likened to a soap opera. J R Ewing, of the long-running TV soap "Dallas", once said: "The cardinal rule of politics: Never get caught in bed with a live man or a dead woman." A rule President George W. Bush, whom Brockie saw as Ewing's double, is bound to have taken to heart.

"Politicians are like prostitutes; full of promise. Their services are also invariably more expensive than helpful." Reg Birchfield, New Zealand journalist-publisher, in *National Business Review* (1978)

"I'm half-Scot, half Maori – there's nobody perfect." Winston Peters, (1946-) leader of New Zealand First party

"The common denominator of MPs is egoism." Sir Wallace (Bill) Rowling, New Zealand Prime Minister (1974-75)

"One has to be a lowbrow, a bit of a murderer, to be a politician, ready and willing to see people sacrificed, slaughtered, for the sake of an idea, whether a good one or a bad one." Henry Miller, US writer (1891-1980)

"I remain just one thing, and one thing only – and that is a clown. It places me on a far higher plane than any politician." English film actor Charlie Chaplin (1889-1977)

"The most successful politician is he who says what everybody else is thinking most often and in the loudest voice." Theodore Roosevelt, US President (1901-09)

But politics do not attract everyone:
"I could never bear to be a politician. I couldn't bear to be right all the time." Sir Peter Ustinov, British actor/writer (1921-2004)

While the ever-acid-tongued H L Mencken also disqualified himself:
"I am strongly in favour of common sense, common honesty and common decency. This makes me forever ineligible for public office."

Jonathan Swift, Irish satirist (1667-1745) had a view when he wrote in *Gulliver's Travels*:
"Whoever could make two ears of corn or two blades of grass to grow upon a spot of ground where only one grew before, would deserve better of mankind, and do more essential service to his country, than the whole race of politicians put together."

And old Aesop knew tellers of fables when he saw them, declaring:
"We hang the petty thieves and appoint the great ones to public office."

Of Don Brash, who overthrew his predecessor Bill English by one vote to snatch the leadership of New Zealand's National Party in October 2003, journalist John Armstrong wrote: "The ex-banker has all the necessary attributes of a politician – blinding ambition and complete disregard for loyalty." Brash then ditched his newly-appointed No.2 Nick Smith after a fortnight in favour of Gerry Brownlee. Brockie depicts all four in a circus setting.

So Are Politicians Honest?

"The only time politicians tell the truth is when they call each other liars."
Bumper sticker popular during the 2004 US presidential election.

"I did not have sexual relations with that woman, Miss Lewinsky."
Bill Clinton US President (1993-2001), the first elected to the office to be impeached in 1998. He later defended his statement, saying that oral sex was not the same as sexual relations.

"Every government is run by liars and nothing they say should be believed."
I F (Issy) Stone (1907-89), US political journalist who founded *I F Stone's Weekly*

"There are only 600 people in the world who have an understanding in depth of the problems of the world economy ... I take some pleasure from being included in that number."
Sir Robert Muldoon, New Zealand Prime Minister and Finance Minister (1975-84), speaking three years after leaving his own country's economy on the brink of ruin at the time of his election defeat.

"A lie is an abomination unto the Lord and a very present help in time of trouble."
Adlai Stevenson, US politician and presidential candidate (1900-65)

"An honest politician is one who, when he is bought, will stay bought."
Simon Cameron, US politician (1799-1889)

"Richard Nixon is a no-good lying bastard. He can lie out of both sides of his mouth at the same time, and if he ever caught himself telling the truth, he'd lie just to keep his hand in."
Harry S Truman, US President 1945-53

"Nixon is the kind of politician who would cut down a redwood tree, then mount the stump for a speech on conservation." Adlai Stevenson

"The proper memory for a politician is one who knows what to remember and what to forget."
Viscount John Morley, British writer-statesman (1838-1923) *Recollections II.*

Sir Robert Muldoon liked to think himself an economic wizard during his nine years as New Zealand's Prime Minister and Finance Minister, boasting: "There are only 600 people in the world who have an understanding in depth of the problems of the world economy ... I take some pleasure from being included in that number." But the country was on the brink of bankruptcy when voters tired of his one-man band.

Cruel & Unusual Punishment

1398

1998

Brockie

Bill Clinton (US President 1993-2001) was the first elected to the office to be impeached (in 1998) after saying: "I did not have sexual relations with that woman, Miss Lewinsky." He later defended his statement, saying that oral sex was not the same as sexual relations. One of Monica Lewinsky's dresses, her underwear, a cigar and the telephone figured in the subsequent scandal, items Brockie included when comparing Clinton to an adulterer in the stocks being pelted with rotten vegetables and stinking fish in the Middle Ages.

"I know all the bad things that happened in the war. I was in uniform for four years myself."
Ronald Reagan, US President (1981–89), defending a visit to Nazi war graves in Germany. Critics pointed out that he spent his time in Hollywood making training films.

"He occasionally stumbled on the truth, but hastily picked himself up and hurried on as if nothing had happened."
Sir Winston Churchill on three-time British PM Stanley Baldwin

MPs cannot accuse each other of lying in Parliament, but Churchill was adept at getting round that convention, replying to Labour foe Aneurin Bevan in the House on December 8, 1944: "I should think it hardly possible to state the opposite of the truth with more precision."

"You don't tell deliberate lies, but sometimes you have to be evasive."
Margaret Thatcher, British PM (1979-90)

"There is just one rule for politicians all over the world. Don't say in power what you say in opposition: if you do, you only have to carry out what the other fellows have found impossible."
John Galsworthy, British novelist (1867-1933)

...Some Too Honest For Their Own Good

"You should always keep something up your sleeve for next year. Keep the bastards on a string and then they'll keep you in office."
Richard "King Dick" Seddon, New Zealand Premier (1893-1906)

... who also said:
"It is unreasonable and unnatural to expect the government to look with the same kindly eye on districts returning members opposed to the government as on those which returned government supporters."

"I am afraid that a lot of things that many of us have said in the past three years are going to have to be unsaid."
Denis Healey, (1917-) British Labour cabinet minister

US President Ronald Reagan visited the graves of Nazi soldiers at Bitburg in May 1985 while on an official visit to Germany to honour war dead, 40 years after the end of World War II. Reagan defended the controversial visit, saying: "I know all the bad things that happened in the war. I was in uniform for four years myself." Critics pointed out that he spent his time in Hollywood making training films.

This is the first time this Brockie cartoon has been published. *The National Business Review* declined to print it at the time, deeming it "too offensive".

"It's a piece of cake until you get to the top. You find you can't stop playing the game the way you've always played it." Richard Nixon

"Since a politician never believes what he says, he is surprised when others believe him." Charles de Gaulle

"If you can't convince them confuse them."
Harry S Truman

"If you want to succeed in politics, you must keep your conscience well under control."
David Lloyd George, British PM (1916-22)

" 'No comment' is a splendid expression. I am using it again and again." Winston Churchill

"The nine most terrifying words in the English language are: 'I'm from the government and I'm here to help.' "
Ronald Reagan

"If it takes a bloodbath, let's get it over with. No more appeasement."
Ronald Reagan, (1970) as Governor of California, suggesting how to deal with student demonstrators.

Robert Askin, premier of New South Wales, told his chauffeur to keep driving when anti-Vietnam war protestors blocked the street, waiting for visiting US President Lyndon Johnson.
"I said: 'Ride over the bastards'," he recalled later. "This comment made me quite popular with the president."

"There are two problems in my life. The political ones are insoluble and the economic ones are incomprehensible."
Alec Douglas-Home, British Conservative PM (1963-64)

"When I call for statistics about the rate of infant mortality, what I want is proof that fewer babies died when I was Prime Minister than when anyone else was Prime Minister. That is a political statistic."
Winston Churchill

US President Abraham Lincoln accepted that "You can fool some of the people all of the time and all of the people some of the time, but you cannot fool all of the people all the time."

Using your democratic right to vote you send your representatives to

Parliament

.... which is "nothing less than a big meeting of more or less idle people", according to Walter Bagehot, British journalist and constitutionalist (1826-77)

"My dear father, only people who look dull ever get into the House of Commons, and only people who are dull ever succeed there." Oscar Wilde

"A great many persons are able to become members of this House without losing their insignificance." Beverley Baxter, (1891-1964) British MP

In the United States, the serpent-tongued H L Mencken said: "Congress consists of one-third, more or less, scoundrels; two-thirds, more or less, idiots; and three-thirds, more or less, poltroons."

... while fellow political cynic Mark Twain (1835-1910) declared:
"It could probably be shown by facts and figures that there is no distinctly native American criminal class except Congress."
... Twain also said:
"Suppose you were an idiot, and suppose you were a member of Congress – but I repeat myself."
... and:
"Fleas can be taught nearly everything a Congressman can."

A later American writer, Mary McCarthy (1912-89) wrote:
"Congress – these for the most part illiterate hacks whose fancy vests are spotted with gravy and whose speeches, hypocritical, unctuous and slovenly, are spotted also with the gravy of political patronage."

While one William "Fishbait" Miller, a retired doorman at the US Congress, recalled:
"80 percent were hypocrites, 80 percent liars, 80 percent serious sinners ... except on Sundays. There is always boozing and floozying ..."

"If I studied all my life, I couldn't think up half the number of funny things passed in one session of Congress."
Will Rogers, US actor-humorist (1879-1935)

In New Zealand, Norman Kirk, Prime Minister (1972-74), dubbed Parliament: "… this intellectually cancerous place. There is too much intrigue and too much dirty, rotten, nasty knife-work for this to be a pleasant place."

Forty years earlier, Labour Party rebel John A Lee said that New Zealand had "… a Parliament of curs".

Charles Dickens summed up the proceedings of Parliament in *Little Dorritt*:
"If another Gunpowder Plot had been discovered half an hour before the lighting of the match, nobody would have been justified in saving the Parliament until there had been half a score of boards, half a bushel of minutes, several sacks of official memoranda, and a family-vault-full of ungrammatical correspondence, on the part of the Circumlocution Office."

"When in that House MPs divide
If they've a brain and cerebellum, too,
They've got to leave that brain outside,
And vote just as their leaders tell 'em too."
Gilbert and Sullivan (*Iolanthe*)

Some countries are not satisfied with one lot of politicians in their parliament … they also have

Upper Houses

In Britain it is the House of Lords, dubbed "the perfect eventide home" by one member,
Baroness Mary Stocks (1891-1975) while another, Baron Donald Soper (1903-98) said:
"… it is good evidence of life after death."

"The House of Lords must be the only institution in the world which is kept efficient by the persistent absenteeism of most of its members."
Herbert Samuel, British Liberal statesman (1870-1963)

In America, the upper house is the Senate, where "Office hours are from 12 to 1 with an hour off for lunch", according to George S. Kaufman, playwright (1889-1961)

… and even one of the inmates, Bob Dole, who was the Republican majority leader (1994-96), confessed: "If you're hanging around with nothing to do and the zoo is closed, come over to the Senate. You'll get the same kind of feeling and you won't have to pay."

And, don't forget that Shakespeare wrote:
"A plague o' both your houses."

Traditionally nobody is more important in Parliament than

Mr Speaker

"There is much exaggeration about the attainments required for a Speaker. All Speakers are highly successful, all Speakers are deeply regretted, and generally announced to be irreplaceable. But a Speaker is soon found, and found, almost invariably, among the mediocrities of the House."
Lord Rosebery, British Prime Minister (1894-95), to Queen Victoria

The Speaker, of course, is completely neutral, but as Tip O'Neill, who steered the US House of Representatives from 1977-87, said:
"I'm against any deal that I'm not in on."

Political Parties

Most politicians do not play politics on their own, of course. They join a party, organisations of which Benjamin Disraeli wrote in *Vivian Grey*, 1824:
"There is no act of treachery or meanness of which a political party is not capable; for in politics there is no honour."

This displayed a cynicism that is clearly international, American comic actor Will Rogers declaring:
"The more you read and observe about politics, you got to admit that each party is worse than the other. The one that's out always looks the best."

"In politics, as on the sickbed, people toss from one side to the other, thinking they will be more comfortable."
Johann Goethe, German writer (1749-1832)

"All political parties die of swallowing their own lies."
Jonathan Swift in *Thoughts on Various Subjects*

"Any party which takes credit for the rain must not be surprised if its opponents blame it for the drought."
Dwight W. Morrow, US politician (1873-1931)

Elections invariably bring about the formation of new parties, each with its own special – and peculiar – sphere of interest. Brockie has got them all here.

"I always voted at my party's call,
And I never thought of thinking for myself at all."
W S Gilbert, *HMS Pinafore*

"More and more I am resolved to be involved in no kind of party politics. Blessed are the Eskimos, who have none."
James Cameron, British foreign correspondent (1911–85)

Some parties are Conservative (or conservative):

A member of which was defined by Ambrose Bierce in *The Devil's Dictionary* as:
"A statesman who is enamoured of existing evils, as distinguished from the Liberal who wishes to replace them with others".

"A Conservative government is an organised hypocrisy." Benjamin Disraeli, English PM who headed two of them.

"The radical invents the views. When he has worn them out, the conservative adopts them."
Mark Twain

"A conservative is a man with two perfectly good legs who, however, has never learned to walk forward."
Franklin D Roosevelt, US Democrat President (1933-45)

"A conservative is someone who believes in reform. But not now."
US comic/satirist Mort Sahl

"I'd ask the Minister whether ... it's appropriate in this case for a woman's body parts to be inserted into a sheep when that's normally been the domain of Tory males ..." Grant Gillon, New Zealand Alliance MP, goes below the belt in debate on genetic engineering of animals.

Some are Socialist or Labour

"A lot of people think I am the Devil reincarnated." Sir Roger Douglas, Finance Minister in the New Zealand Labour Government elected in 1984 and architect of Rogernomics which spurned traditional socialism in favour of radical economic reform.

A Labour administration was cruelly described by the Conservative Winston Churchill as "Government of the duds, for the duds, by the duds".

"A lot of people think I'm the Devil reincarnated," said Sir Roger Douglas, Finance Minister in a New Zealand Labour government and architect of Rogernomics which spurned traditional Socialism in favour of radical economic reform. Brockie saw Douglas consuming the NZ Labour Party.

"The typical socialist ... a prim little man with a white collar job, usually a secret teetotaller and often with vegetarian leanings".
George Orwell, English writer (1903-50) in *The Road to Wigan Pier*

"What a genius the Labour Party has for cutting itself in half and letting the two parts writhe in public."
William Connor (Cassandra), British newspaper columnist (1910-67)

"The political problem in terms of the party is that we are emotionally crippled – we will go and search for the last victim rather than celebrate the thousandth success."
David Lange, New Zealand Prime Minister (1984-89)

"There is nothing in socialism that a little age or a little money will not cure."
Will Durant, US philosopher (1885-1982) or,
as British politician Sir Richard Marsh put it in 1976:
"As far as socialism means anything, it must be about the wider distribution of smoked salmon and caviar."

But Harold Wilson, British Labour Party leader and two-time Prime Minister (1964-70), (74-76), had modest tastes ...
"If I had the choice between smoked salmon and tinned salmon, I'd have it tinned. With vinegar."

Wilson also said:
"The Labour Party is like a stagecoach. If you rattle along at great speed everybody inside is too exhilarated or too seasick to cause any trouble. But if you stop everybody gets out and argues about where to go next."

"Any man who is not something of a socialist before he is 40 has no heart. Any man who is still a socialist after he is 40 has no head."
Wendell Wilkie, US businessman drafted as unsuccessful Republican presidential candidate in 1940

"I am a Socialist – and I only wish the Labour Party was."
Baron Donald Soper

"I am tired of feeling like the man with the broom and shovel following the Labour elephant. Principles come first and if there is conflict between principles and party, then principles must win."
Mike Moore, New Zealand Labour Prime Minister (1990)

... Some Liberal or liberal

"As usual, the Liberals offer a mixture of sound and original ideas. Unfortunately, none of the sound ideas is original and none of the original ideas is sound."
Harold Macmillan, British Conservative Prime Minister (1957-63)

"If God had been a Liberal, we wouldn't have had the Ten Commandments - we'd have the Ten Suggestions."
Malcolm Bradbury, British writer (1932-2000)

"A liberal is a man too broadminded to take his own side in a quarrel."
Robert Frost, US poet (1874-1963)

... or "a man who leaves the room before the fight begins," in the view of American wit Heywood Broun (1888-1939)

... A view confirmed perhaps by Jo Grimond who led the British Liberal Party in 1958:
"Liberals must give up being so excessively respectable. We must have some bloody noses in the party."

... And "It must be said about the Liberals that they would give a standing ovation to anyone reading out the telephone book, if it were read in terms of decent moderation. They are a wonderul lot."
James Cameron

And in Britain, there was the
Monster Raving Loony Party,

of whom astronomer/writer Patrick Moore said:
"They had one advantage over all the other parties. They knew they were loonies."

Robert Muldoon, New Zealand National Party Prime Minister (1975-84), ruled the country and his party like a dictator. He still tried to call the shots when ousted as party leader after losing the 1984 election to Labour's David Lange, who said later: "They couldn't, in the National Party, run a bath, and if either the deputy leader or the leader tried to, Sir Robert would run away with the plug." This cartoon after he died was rejected by *The National Business Review* after Brockie had abandoned his first effort showing Muldoon being turned away from Hell with the Devil observing that he was too hot to handle. "I must be getting soft in my old age," Brockie said, after elevating Muldoon.

The Opposition

David Lange, New Zealand Labour Party leader who ended the dictatorial Sir Robert Muldoon's nine-year reign with his conservative National Party in 1984, was merciless on his opponents in Opposition.
He demolished Muldoon's successor Jim McLay with remarks like:
"The present Leader of the Opposition would go into a hot flush if he had to pick three pizza toppings out of four."

… and "One swallow does not make a summer and one turkey does not make a Leader of the Opposition."

… and as Muldoon still tried to call the shots, Lange said:
"They couldn't, in the National Party, run a bath, and if either the deputy leader or the leader tried, Sir Robert would run away with the plug."

Of his political opponents, Lange said:
"If they stop telling lies about me, I will stop telling the truth about them."
… and on being ordered in Parliament to withdraw a claim that the Opposition were "bananas", Lange said:
"I withdraw and apologise. I have an affection for that fruit."

"Mr Tierney, a great Whig authority, used always to say that the duty of an opposition was very simple – it was to oppose everything and propose nothing."
Lord Stanley, a 19th century English historian and clergyman.

Ambrose Bierce, in *The Devil's Dictionary*, defined Opposition as:
"In politics, the party that prevents the government from running amok by hamstringing it."

But G K Chesterton, British writer (1874-1936) wrote:
"English experience indicates that when the two great political parties agree about something it is generally wrong."

"Manipulate is what the other joker does. Organise or strategise is what you do. If the other fella does it, it's a jack-up; if you do it, it's pure democracy."
Mike Moore

"We won. You lost. Eat That."
Michael Cullen, New Zealand Deputy Prime Minister, reminds the Opposition of political reality.

Independents
insist on staying out of party politics

... or as Adlai Stevenson put it:
"An independent is a guy who wants to take the politics out of politics."

"Independence is in the mind of a man, or it is nowhere ... No minister can expect to find in me a servile vassal. No minister can expect from me the abandonment of any principle I have avowed, or any pledge I have given."
Richard Brinsley Sheridan, playwright (1751-1816), who spent 32 years in the British Parliament, all but two very brief periods in opposition.

Politicians and Alcohol

"This country will not be run over a whisky bottle ..."
Jenny Shipley after ousting Jim Bolger to become New Zealand's first woman Prime Minister in November 1997. This was a dig at Bolger's reported late-night, spirit-fuelled, policy-making sessions with his coalition partner and Deputy Prime Minister Winston Peters.

Shipley (Prime Minister 1997-99), who said at the time: "I've been seen to hold a sherry in my hand or indeed a gin and tonic, but I generally don't drink when I'm working," then sacked Peters, ending the coalition, in August 1998.

Tariana Turia, rebel New Zealand Labour Party minister turned independent, was subject to an attack in Parliament by Peters who accused her of over-indulging in fast food. She responded:
"I don't think that I need to account to Mr Peters for my eating habits. Nor do I expect him to account to me for his drinking habits."

Politics and alcohol have long tended to mix, as John Condliffe, a New Zealand-American academic, once wrote, observing that the House of Representatives' "alcoholic average was greater than its intellectual average".

"I have taken more out of alcohol than alcohol has taken out of me."
Winston Churchill, who also said ...
"When I was younger, I made it a rule never to take strong drink before lunch and now it is my rule never to do so before breakfast."

The situation was no different in the US Congress, as Mark Twain observed:
"Whisky is carried into committee rooms in demijohns and carried out in demagogues."

Bessie Braddock, British MP:
"Sir Winston, you are drunk!"
Sir Winston Churchill: "And you madam are ugly. But I shall be sober in the morning."

"Until he emerged from Illinois they always put the women, children and clergy to bed when he got a few gourds of corn aboard ..."
H L Mencken of Abraham Lincoln

"Alcohol is a very necessary article. It enables Parliament to do things at eleven at night that no sane person would do at eleven in the morning."
George Bernard Shaw

"Most British statesmen have either drunk too much or womanised too much. I never fell into the second category."
Lord George Brown, British Labour politician (1914–85)

Politicians On Each Other

Formally in Parliament, they call each other "Honourable Member", but this nicety often disguises an acid-tongued politician, none more than economist Baron John Maynard Keynes, who said of British Prime Minister David Lloyd George:
"This goat-footed bard, this half-human visitor to our age from the hag-ridden magic and enchanted woods of Celtic antiquity".

Lloyd George could also dish it out, as evidenced by his statement about a fellow Liberal Parliamentarian:
"When they circumcised Herbert Samuel they threw away the wrong bit."

"He does not have to somersault all the time just because he lives in a political circus."
David Lange, New Zealand Prime Minister, on former National Party leader Robert Muldoon.

Lange described a subsequent Opposition leader, Jim Bolger, as:
"An itinerant masseur, massaging politically erogenous zones" ... and said on another occasion:
"When he went to the doctor, they sought a second opinion from a vet."

"I'm thoroughly pleased and delighted I've got nothing to do with them."
Winston Peters, leader of New Zealand First, speaking of the National Party before the 1996 election. After the election he joined them in a coalition to form the government.

"It is gratifying to see the country's snot-nosed political elite huffily denounce me ... it is uplifting to see these sickly white liberals deciding for the rest of us what is in good taste ..."
Winston Peters again – on just about everyone else.

"An empty taxi arrived and Mr Atlee got out ...
A modest little man with much to be modest about."
Winston Churchill

"In the depths of that dusty soul is nothing but abject surrender."
Winston Churchill on Neville Chamberlain

"Mr (Joseph) Chamberlain loves the working man – he loves to see him work."
Winston Churchill

New Zealand Labour Prime Minister David Lange toppled his National Party predecessor Robert Muldoon in 1984 after cracks like "He does not have to somersault all the time just because he lives in a political circus."

My relationship with the National Party is strange & wonderful...

They're strange...

& I'm wonderful.

Winston Peters, leader of the New Zealand First party, dismissed his former colleagues in the National Party in the run-up to the 1996 election, saying: "I'm thoroughly pleased and delighted I've got nothing to do with them." After the election, he joined them in a coalition to form the government.

"The right honourable gentleman is indebted to his memory for his jests and to his imagination for his facts."
Richard Brinsley Sheridan, of cabinet minister Henry Dundas

"The know-nothing PM supported by the do-nothing Finance Minister."
John A Lee, rebel New Zealand Labour MP, on Michael Joseph Savage and Walter Nash (1937)
... and on Savage's government:
"A Cabinet of incompetents presided over by the most incompetent."

"I heard his library burned down and that both books were destroyed – and one of them hadn't even been coloured in yet."
John Dawkins, Australian MP on fellow member Wilson Tuckey

"He is a man of splendid abilities, but utterly corrupt. Like rotten mackerel by moonlight, he shines and stinks."
US Senator John Randolph of Roanoke (1773-1883), of fellow politician Edward Livingston

"If a traveller were informed that such a man was leader of the House of Commons he may begin to comprehend how the Egyptians worshipped an insect."
Benjamin Disraeli of Lord John Russell, who also became Britain's PM twice.

While John Bright, statesman and orator (1811-89), said of Disraeli:
"He is a self-made man, and worships his creator."

Winston Churchill was withering in his descriptions of Labour Party contemporary Sir Stafford Cripps, of whom he said:
"There, but for the grace of God, goes God."... and
"He has all of the virtues I dislike and none of the vices I admire."

But Cripps' Labour colleague Aneurin Bevan had his own views on Churchill, saying:
"The Prime Minister has got very many virtues and, when the time comes, I hope to pay my tribute to them, but I am bound to say that political honesty and sagacity have never been among them."

"You look like an Easter Island statue with an arse-full of razor blades."
Australian Labor Party leader Paul Keating's endearment to Liberal PM Malcolm Fraser ...

... while Keating's predecessor Bob Hawke said:
"Malcolm Fraser could be described as a cutlery man – he was born with a silver spoon in his mouth and he uses it to stab his colleagues in the back."

"He has all the characteristics of a dog – except loyalty."
Sam Houston, US senator and soldier, of a certain Thomas Jefferson Green

New Zealand Prime Minister David Lange on British counterpart John Major after he had succeeded Margaret Thatcher:
"He has stayed the axe Mrs Thatcher was about to take to the National Health Service, observing that his parents had the benefit of it. Britons may soon wish that his parents had travelled by train or used electricity."

Women Politicians

Margaret Thatcher, British PM (1979-90), was described by her biographer John Campbell as "not merely the first woman and the longest-serving Prime Minister of modern times, but the most admired, most hated, most idolised, most vilified public figure of the second half of the 20th century." It is inevitable that she should dominate any section on female politicians.

"She is the Castro of the Western world – an embarrassment to her friends – all she lacks is a beard."
Former Labour cabinet minister Lord Healey

"She ate a television journalist for breakfast and, feeling peckish, bit off some reporters' heads at a press conference."
British journalist Trevor Fishlock

"I cannot bring myself to vote for a woman who has been voice-trained to speak to me as though my dog has just died."
British writer Keith Waterhouse (1929-)

Mrs Thatcher was renowned as the "toughest man" in her Cabinet. She said in 1980:

Visiting New Zealand before the 1987 general election, Geoffrey Howe, British Foreign Secretary, made public references linking the anti-nuclear policy with trade to Europe which Prime Minister David Lange saw as undiplomatic interference in his country's domestic affairs. Brockie depicted Margaret Thatcher's pleasure as the Howe bulldog lifted his leg over Lange and Cabinet colleagues.

"I don't mind how much my ministers talk – as long as they do what I say."

Despite being a grocer's daughter, she was not renowned for the common touch. As Education Minister, with the British economy worsening daily in 1970, she observed:
"Most of us have stopped using silver every day."

Jenny Shipley was described as "the most hated minister in the history of New Zealand" when she slashed benefits in 1991 as Minister of Social Welfare in the conservative National Party government. Shipley responded:
"Being hated is not the important thing. Doing what is right is important."

When Shipley went on to become the country's first woman Prime Minister, former MP Michael Laws commented on her toughness as follows:
"Jenny can tell you in wonderful warm tones how she's going to garrotte you and then disembowel you and throw your intestines over her left shoulder. She never raises her voice but the assault is deadly."

"I say if you give (them) too much power you unsex women."
Richard Seddon, New Zealand Prime Minister, who also said:
"By granting the franchise to women, Parliament plunged into an abyss of unknown depth."

Responding to a newspaper editorial that said New Zealanders like their leaders to be ordinary, like them, Helen Clark, elected Prime Minister of a Labour Party-led coalition in 1999, said:
"For God's sake – I am not prepared to make myself ordinary. If ordinary means I have suddenly got to produce a household of kids and iron (husband) Peter's shirts, I'm sorry, I'm not interested."

Clark said:
"If I hadn't got into politics, I would not have got married …"
Twenty years later, she said the anniversary would be celebrated with a telephone call, adding:
"I'm in Wellington being Prime Minister. He's in Christchurch being professor of public health. That's probably why it's lasted 20 years."

Jenny Shipley, widely seen as New Zealand's Margaret Thatcher, was a silent menacer who would have put a human face to the Spanish Inquisition, said ex-MP Michael Laws. "Jenny can tell you in wonderful warm tones how she's going to garrotte you and then disembowel you and throw your intestines over her left shoulder. She never raises her voice but the assault is deadly." Brockie depicted her bent on improving her MPs' behaviour in Parliament.

Dead Politicians

"How do they know?" Dorothy Parker, US writer (1893-1967) asked when told the un-charismatic former US President Calvin Coolidge had passed away in 1933.

"I did not attend his funeral, but I sent a letter saying I approved of it."
Mark Twain, of a demised Congressman.

"We had three brandies each, to celebrate Savage's death. There was no regret. Those present, a caucus majority, decided that, in dying, Savage had made his first intelligent gesture ... "
John A. Lee, New Zealand Labour MP (1931–43) on his leader Michael Joseph Savage, who was not in fact dead. Lee added: "I got the report wrong. The brandy was wasted, for we are a dry lot."

And Not Dead, But Ex-Politicians?

David Lange, ex-New Zealand Prime Minister, said:
"The only sensible way to leave the job as Prime Minister was by a state funeral. You had rehabilitation immediately, you became a legend in your bedtime and you got the whole thing paid for."

Lange, who did not die in office but resigned, described his own time as Prime Minister as "fleeting, transient ... on the wallpaper of history I'm a flyspeck."

Some politicians fall foul of their parties and are cast off. Lange said they could have an afterlife:
"After the event, the fallen is exhumed, honoured, and becomes an international consultant on economic matters (God knows, haven't the Poles suffered enough?) Or else is given a diplomatic posting."

"I think Ian Botham is the stuff of which heroes are made. I have certain soul sympathy for him, because sportsmen and politicians suffer the same fate. All their successes are written in sand and their failures are carved in stone."
Neil Kinnock, British Labour Party leader, who failed to win an election.

"All political lives, unless they are cut-off in mid-stream at a happy juncture, end in failure."
Enoch Powell, British MP (1912-98), who was sacked by the Conservative Party and finally lost his seat as an Ulster Unionist.

"Anyone who says four times, he isn't going to resign, definitely will."
John Kenneth Galbraith

"What this country needs is more unemployed politicians."
Angela Davis, US revolutionary and writer (1944-)

The Candidates

"He knows nothing; and he thinks he knows everything. That points clearly to a political career."
George Bernard Shaw in *Major Barbara*

"In politics we must choose between the strong man, whose real interests are elsewhere and who will leave office the moment bigger opportunity beckons, and the weakling who will cling because he can't hold a job anywhere else. Public office is the last refuge of the incompetent."
Boise Penrose, US writer in *Collier's Weekly* (1931)

"Of course, in my country most political leaders are, well, not gangsters, but more or less the same kind of thing. I mean, people who go in for getting elected, what can you expect of men like that?"
Jorge Luis Borges, Argentinian writer (1899-1986).

"The saddest life is that of a political aspirant under democracy. His failure is ignominious and his success is disgraceful." H L Mencken

When an unsuccessful Tory candidate changed parties to stand for the Liberals, Winston Churchill said it was the "only recorded case in history of a rat swimming towards a sinking ship".

Proportional Representation

New Zealand's voting system called Mixed Member Proportional (MMP) has produced coalition governments since it was introduced in 1996. David Lange, Labour Prime Minister in 1984-89, who had no time for the Greens in particular, commented later: "I could never have operated with MMP. I couldn't bear to be consulting people I regard as off the planet."

"Proportional Representation, I think, is fundamentally counter-democratic."
Neil Kinnock, former British Labour Party leader, who did not win an election under the first-past-the-post voting system.

In Canada, journalist Larry Zolf said of coalitions:
"For Socialists, going to bed with the Liberals is like having oral sex with a shark."

Long-time politicians like to think of themselves as

Statesmen

"A politician is a person with whose politics you don't agree. If you agree with him, he is a statesman."
David Lloyd George, British Prime Minister (1916-22)

"A statesman is a politician who's been dead 10 or 15 years."
Harry S Truman

"A politician is a statesman who approaches every question with an open mouth."
Adlai Stevenson

"You can always get the truth from an American statesman after he has turned 70, or given up all hope of the presidency."
Wendell Phillips, US reformer and orator (1811-84)

"A politician thinks of the next election; a statesman, of the next generation."
James Freeman Clarke, US clergyman (1810-88)

Meanwhile...MMP has driven MPs to assume unnatural postures

brockie

In New Zealand's experience, the Mixed Member Proportional (MMP) form of government, which makes coalitions inevitable, has forced Members of Parliament to assume unnatural postures, as Brockie shows.

"The difference between being an elder statesman and posing successfully as an elder statesman is practically negligible."
T S Eliot, poet and playwright (1888-1965) in *The Elder Statesman*

Political Wit

... sadly, a declining feature of contemporary life, but politics have been getting boring for half a century, as Adlai Stevenson observed in the 1950s:
"I suppose maybe it's the general quality of banality or conventionality that's crept into our political dialogue. Generally speaking, the standardisation of talk, of newspaper reporting and the kind of banality of most of the television programmes have created a standard of manners which is deprived of a good deal of lusty vigour, especially of the use of wit and humour that we used to have."

Happily, there are one or two exceptions, notably David Lange, Prime Minister of New Zealand (1984-89) whose anti-nuclear policy provoked the US into withdrawing his country's age-old ally status.
Lange told retiring American ambassador H. Monroe Browne, who had a racehorse called Lacka Reason:

"You must be the only ambassador in the world to own a horse named after his country's foreign policy."

The anti-nuclear policy was persistently attacked by senior officers of the US Navy, including Admiral Crowe, its Commander-in-Chief in the Pacific, and Lange made the following response in 1993:
"Given that the US is the world's remaining super-power it might, on the face of it, give concern that retired US Admiral Crowe has been appointed chairman of President (Bill) Clinton's Foreign Intelligence Advisory Board. However, it is plain that this appointment is a reward for political support during the presidential campaign and not an admission that Admiral Crowe has any intelligence."
His statement ended: "Mr Lange wished the admiral well in his career as a novelist."

Lange was never slow to use his wit on critics who wrote often illiterate letters attacking him or his government's policies. This is the complete text of one letter he wrote in reply:
"I turned over a rock this morning and found underneath it, stridulating with malice and swaggering in ignorance, a teacher who couldn't spell. I put the rock back in its place."

New Zealand's mid-1980s' anti-nuclear policy banning visits by nuclear-armed and nuclear-powered ships, incensed its traditional ally, the United States, which effectively threw it out of the ANZUS alliance, stopped military cooperation and suspended top-level political contacts. Brockie captured US and President Ronald Reagan's pique in these two cartoons depicting the American political and military reaction.

Lord Sandwich: " 'Pon my honour, Wilkes. I don't know whether you'll die on the gallows or of the pox."
John Wilkes: "That must depend, my Lord, upon whether I embrace your lordship's principles, or your lordship's mistress."

Lady Astor: "If you were my husband, I should flavour your coffee with poison."
Winston Churchill: "Madam, if you were my wife, I should drink it."

"Mr Speaker, I said the honourable member was a liar it is true and I am sorry for it. The honourable member may place the punctuation where he pleases."
Richard Brinsley Sheridan

"Greater love hath no man than this, that he lay down his friends for his life."
Jeremy Thorpe, leader of the British Liberal Party, on Prime Minister Harold Macmillan's 1962 purge of the Cabinet when he sacked six ministers, known as "The Night of the Long Knives".

Politicians On the Press

"I believe that nothing in the newspapers is ever true – and that is why they are so popular, the taste of the age being decidedly for fiction."
Benjamin Disraeli

"I read the newspaper avidly. It is my one form of continuous fiction."
Aneurin Bevan, British Labour politician (1897-1960)

"The newspapers! Sir, they are the most villainous - licentious – abominable – infernal – Not that I ever read them – No – I make it a rule never to look into a news-paper."
Richard Brinsley Sheridan

David Lange on press conferences:
"The only reason television is there, they hope I'll pick my nose. They certainly don't carry any substance of what is said."

Not all politicians have been hostile to the press.
"Were it left to me to decide whether we should have a government without newspapers or newspapers without government, I should not hesitate a moment

to prefer the latter."
Thomas Jefferson, US President (1801-09)

"Freedom of conscience, of education, of speech, of assembly are among the very fundamentals of democracy and all of them would be nullified should freedom of the press ever be successfully challenged."
Franklin D Roosevelt, US President (1933-45)

Sir Philip Francis (1740-1818) a British MP who wrote on politics under the pseudonym Junius, said it all on this subject:
"Let it be impressed upon your minds, let it be installed into your children, that the liberty of the press is the palladium of all the civil, political and religious rights."

The Press On Politicians

"The relationship between the press and politicians should be similar to that between dogs and lamp posts."
H L Mencken

"Candidly speaking, the average politician is not a very interesting gentleman to meet. He is usually utterly devoid of imagination, he is mercenary, selfish and one-eyed."
Pat Lawlor, New Zealand journalist-writer (1893–1979)

"In Mexico, an air-conditioner is called a politician because it makes a lot of noise but doesn't work very well." Len Deighton, British writer (1929-)

"Democracy becomes a government of bullies tempered by editors."
Ralph Waldo Emerson, US poet-essayist (1803-82)

"Politicians can forgive almost anything in the way of abuse; they can forgive subversion, revolution, being contradicted, exposed as liars, even ridiculed but they can never forgive being ignored."
Auberon Waugh, British writer-critic (1939- 2001)

"Any political party that can't cough up anything better than a treacherous brain-damaged old vulture like Hubert Humphrey deserves every beating it can get. They don't hardly make 'em like Hubert anymore – but just to be on the safe side, he should be castrated anyway."
Hunter S Thompson, US journalist (1939-)

Hail To The Chief

The Presidency of the United States, the most powerful position in the world, was defined by Ambrose Bierce in *The Devil's Dictionary* as:
"The greased pig in the field game of American politics"

H L Mencken marvelled that it was "so fought for by fugitives from the sewers".

And actor-comedian Mel Brooks said: "If presidents don't do it to their wives they do it to the country."

"The presidency is now a cross between a popularity contest and a high school debate, with an encyclopaedia of clichés the first prize." Saul Bellow, US writer (1915-)

"Anyone who wants to be president should have his head examined."
Averell Harriman, US statesman and diplomat (1891-1986)

"Anybody that wants the presidency so much that he'll spend two years organising and campaigning for it, is not to be trusted with the office."
David Broder, Washington political correspondent

George W. Bush depicted as a *Blazing Saddles* sheriff by Brockie, had some difficulty raising international support for his invasion of Iraq. He may yet be best remembered for his subsequent remark: "We have not yet found the stockpiles of weapons that we thought were there."

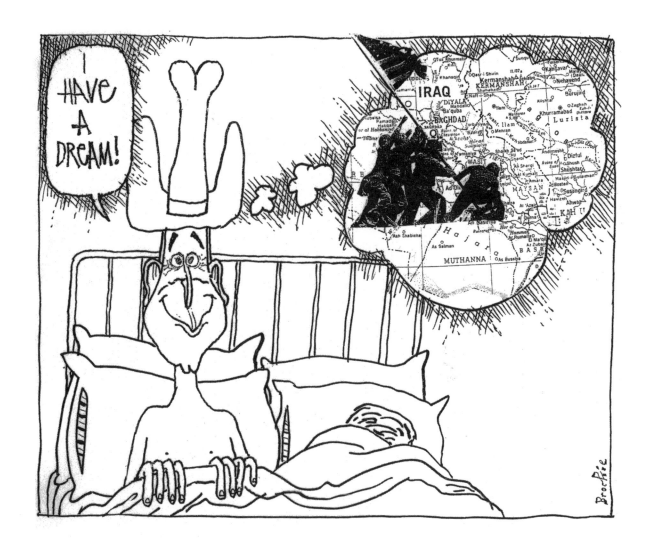

"I sit here all day trying to persuade people to do the things they ought to have sense enough to do without my persuading them ... That's all the powers of a president amount to."
Harry S Truman who had the job 1945-53

H L Mencken said of Calvin Coolidge, who was in the White House from 1923-29: "He slept more than any other president, whether by day or night. Nero fiddled, but Coolidge only snored."

This was a condition also observed by political columnist Walter Lippman who wrote:
"Mr Coolidge's genius for inactivity is developed to a very high point. It is far from being an indolent activity. It is a grim, determined, alert inactivity which keeps Mr Coolidge occupied constantly ... Inactivity is a political philosophy and a party programme with Mr Coolidge."

Such comments did not worry Coolidge who defended himself, saying:
"I think the American people wants a solemn ass as a president, and I think I'll go along with them."

While Lyndon Johnson (who occupied the White House 1963-69) would have welcomed some inactivity, once yearning:
"I wish I could be like an animal in the forest – go to sleep under a tree, eat when I feel like it, read a bit and after a while, do whatever I want to do."

Warren Harding (President 1921-23) did not find the White House job too demanding, saying:
"I love to meet people. It is the most pleasant thing I do. It really is the only fun I have. It does not tax me and it seems to be a very great pleasure to them."

H L Mencken dismissed Harding as "a tin-horn politician with the manner of a rural corn-doctor and the mien of a ham actor".

Mencken, who loved the language, also wrote of Harding:
"He writes the worst English that I have ever encountered. It reminds me of a string of wet sponges; it reminds me of tattered washing on the line; it reminds me of stale bean soup, of college yells, of dogs barking through endless nights. It is so bad a sort of grandeur creeps into it. It drags itself out of the dark

abysm of pish, and crawls insanely up the topmost pinnacle of tosh. It is rumble and bumble. It is flap and doodle. It is balder and dash."

... and of Franklin D Roosevelt, he wrote:
"If he became convinced tomorrow that coming out for cannibalism would get him the votes he sorely needs, he would begin fattening a missionary in the White House backyard come Wednesday."

... while Lord (Conrad) Black, businessman and newspaper owner, wrote of Roosevelt:
"... his techniques, while bloodless, were not always much less ruthless, devious and cynical than Hitler's or Stalin's ... But in applying his ruthless and often amoral physical genius to almost wholly desirable ends, he was a greater statesman than even his greatest supporters have appreciated."

Betty Ford, wife of President Gerald Ford, said wistfully:
"I wish I'd married a plumber. At least he'd be home by five o'clock."

And Lyndon Johnson said memorably (but often quoted with a cruder variation) of Ford:

"Gerry's the only man I ever knew who can't walk and chew gum at the same time."

Dwight Eisenhower (President 1953-61) was easily pleased, saying:
"There is one thing about being president. Nobody can tell you when to sit down."

"I would not like to be a Russian leader - they never know when they're being taped."
US President Richard Nixon, who said after his resignation over Watergate:
"My own view was that the taping of conversations for historical purposes was a bad decision."

George W Bush, elected president in 2000, became famous for his malapropisms with entire websites set up to record them, such as:
"It's clearly a budget. It's got a lot of numbers in it," and ...
"One of the things we've got to make sure that we do is anything."

Bush also memorably said:
"I've been to war. I've raised twins. If I had a choice, I'd rather go to war."

But after invading Iraq in 2003, he may yet be best remembered for:
"We have not yet found the stockpiles of weapons that we thought were there."

... and Vice-Presidents

"Democracy means that anyone can grow up to be President, and anyone who doesn't grow up can be Vice-President."
Johnny Carson, US TV host (1925-)

Dan Quayle, Vice-President to George Bush (1989-92), was widely held to demonstrate that, with British comic John Cleese saying: "If life were fair, Dan Quayle would be making a living asking: 'Do you want fries with that?' "

Quayle's speeches did nothing to dispel that image, as in:
"We offer the party as a big tent. How we do that, with the platform, the preamble to the platform or whatnot, that remains to be seen. But that message will have to be articulated with great clarity."

"All that Hubert needs over there is a gal to answer the phone and a pencil with an eraser on it."
US President Lyndon Johnson on Hubert Humphrey, his deputy in 1964-68

Governments

"To be governed is to be watched, inspected, spied upon, directed, law-ridden, regulated, penned up, indoctrinated, preached at, checked, appraised, seized, censured, commanded, by beings who have neither title, nor knowledge, nor virtue.
"To be governed is to have every operation, every transaction, every movement noted, registered, counted, rated, stamped, measured, numbered, assessed, licensed, refused, authorised, endorsed, admonished, prevented, reformed, redressed, corrected."
Pierre Joseph Proudhon, French revolutionary (1809-65)

"No government has ever been, or can ever be, wherein time-servers and blockheads will not be uppermost."
John Dryden, English poet (1631-1700)

"I love my country — it's the government I'm afraid of."
Bumper sticker in 2004 US presidential election.

"The single most exciting thing you encounter in

government is competence, because it's so rare."
Daniel Patrick Moynihan, US diplomat and senator
(1927-)

"There is no government without mumbo-jumbo."
Hilaire Belloc

"The worst government is the most moral. One composed of cynics is often very tolerant and human. But when fanatics are on top there is no limit to oppression." H L Mencken

"Too bad that all the people who know how to run the country are busy driving taxicabs and cutting hair."
George Burns, US comedian (1896-1996)

"I would not give half a guinea to live under one form of government rather than another. It is of no moment to the happiness of the individual."
Dr Samuel Johnson

"Government, even in its best state, is but a necessary evil; in its worst state, an intolerable one."
Thomas Paine, Anglo-American political theorist (1737-1809)

"Government is an association of men who do violence to the rest of us."
Leo Tolstoy, Russian writer (1828-1910)

"I don't make jokes - I just watch the government and report the facts." Will Rogers

"The object of government in peace and in war is not the glory of rulers or of races, but the happiness of the common man."
Baron William Beveridge, British economist and social reformer (1879-1963)

"Governments never learn. Only people learn."
Milton Friedman, US economist (1912-)

"The only good government ... is a bad one in a hell of a fright."
Joyce Cary, British author (1888-1957)

"My experience in government is that when things are non-controversial and beautifully coordinated, there is not much going on."
John F Kennedy

"All free governments are managed by the combined wisdom and folly of the people."
James Garfield, US president briefly in 1881 before being assassinated

"The pleasure of governing must certainly be exquisite if we may judge from the vast numbers who are eager to be concerned with it."
Voltaire, French writer (1694–1778)

... who also said:
"In general, the art of government consists in taking as much money as possible from one party of the citizens to give to the other."

... and "Nine-tenths of the activities of a modern government are harmful. Therefore the worse they are performed the better."

"The art of governing consists in not letting men grow old in their jobs."
Napoleon Bonaparte (*Maxims*)

"All governments are pretty much alike, with a tendency on the part of the last to be the worst."
Sir Austen Chamberlain, British politician (1863–1937)

"In the long run every government is the exact symbol of its people, with their wisdom and unwisdom."
Thomas Carlyle, Scottish writer (1795–1881)

As Joseph de Maistre, an 18th century French diplomat, said:
"Each country has the government it deserves."

And Phaedrus, a 1st century translator of *Aesop's Fables*, observed:
"In a change of government, the poor seldom change anything except the name of their master."

Power

"Nothing is more gratifying to the mind of man than power or dominion."
Joseph Addison, British essayist and politician (1672-1719)

But sometimes power has to be shared, as New Zealand National Party leader Jim Bolger, who liked to see himself as The Great Helmsman of the Ship of State, found after the 1990 election when he was forced to form a coalition with Winston Peters' New Zealand First party. Eventually, the coalition began to fall apart.

"Power tends to corrupt and absolute power corrupts absolutely. Great men are almost always bad men. There is no worse heresy than that the office sanctifies the holder of it."
Lord Acton, 19th century English historian.

But George Bernard Shaw wrote:
"Power does not corrupt man; fools, however, if they get into a position of power, corrupt power."

"Those who have once been intoxicated with power, and have derived any kind of emolument from it, even though but for one year, never can willingly abandon it."

Edmund Burke, 18th century British statesman

... as Napoleon Bonaparte confessed:
"Power is my mistress. I have worked too hard at her conquest to allow anyone to take her away from me, or even to covet her."

"As long as men worship the Caesars and Napoleons, Caesars and Napoleons will duly rise and make them desirable."
Aldous Huxley, English writer (1894-1963).

"Apart from the occasional saint, it is difficult for people who have the smallest amount of power to be nice."
Dr Anthony Clare, Irish psychiatrist and broadcaster

"The truth is that prime ministers are not as powerful as some of the public imagine. Nor are ministers. As Minister of Education I received a number of letters from school children asking me to sack their teachers. To a child they started with a cunning reference to their support for the anti-nuclear policy. Now the simple fact was ... our system of government, sadly but sensibly, does not afford any minister that power."
David Lange

Above all, politicians desire power. But sometimes power has to be shared, as New Zealand National Party leader Jim Bolger, who liked to see himself as The Great Helmsman of the Ship of State, found after the 1990 election when he was forced to form a coalition with Winston Peters' New Zealand First party. Eventually the coalition began to fall apart and some members jumped overboard, as Brockie graphically depicted.

The Great Helmsman

"Nothing is more gratifying to the mind of a man than power or dominion," wrote British politician Joseph Addison. U.S. President George W. Bush looked pretty gratified when he boasted "Mission Accomplished" after toppling Saddam Hussein. but there was a downside, as Brockie depicted in this cartoon.

63

"We often say how impressive power is. But I do not find it impressive at all. The guns and the bombs, the rockets and the warships, are all symbols of human failure. They are necessary symbols. They protect what we cherish. But they are witness to human folly."
Lyndon Johnson, US president (1963-69), whose unpopular escalation of the Vietnam War led to his retirement.
... but power to Johnson also meant demanding loyalty. Issuing guidelines for White House staff, he said:
"I want him to kiss my ass in Macy's window at high noon and tell me it smells like roses. I want his pecker in my pocket."

"No man is good enough to govern another man without that other's consent."
Abraham Lincoln, US president (1861-65)

Power, of course, includes what US Senator John Randolph called:
"That most delicious of all privileges – spending other people's money."

Political Speeches ...

Asked why she insisted on writing her own speeches, New Zealand Prime Minister Helen Clark said:
"We could not afford a speech-writer who could write to my specifications."

Every politician likes to think his speech is the one that is quickly going to change the nation, or the course of history. In fact, as British MP Robert Boothby observed in 1936:
"If from any speech in the House one begins to see any results within five to 10 years after it has been delivered, one will have done very well indeed."

"Mr Lloyd George (British PM) spoke for a hundred and seventeen minutes, in which period he was detected only once in the use of an argument."
Arnold Bennett, English writer (1867-1931)

"He is one of those orators of whom it was well said, 'Before they get up they do not know what they are going to say; when they are speaking, they do not know what they are saying; and when they sit down, they do not know what they have said'."
Winston Churchill, of fellow MP and naval commander Lord Charles Beresford

... Churchill, a great orator, was once described by another politician as having "devoted the best years of his life to preparing his impromptu speeches".

... as Mark Twain observed:
"It usually takes more than three weeks to prepare a good impromptu speech."

"I dreamt I was making a speech in the House. I woke up, and by Jove I was!"
Duke of Devonshire, English politician.

"Boys, I may not know much, but I know chicken shit from chicken salad."
Lyndon B Johnson, on a speech by then US Vice-President Richard Nixon in the Senate.

Of a budget by political opponent Ruth Richardson, New Zealand Prime Minister David Lange wrote:
"Its well practised recitations, its every swivel

New Zealand Prime Minister Helen Clark, at full cry in this Brockie cartoon, is not only one of her Parliament's most forceful speakers, she also writes her own speeches. "We could not afford a speech-writer who could write to my specifications," she said.

choreographed by some demented elocution teacher to competition society standard, could not disguise its banality."

"Hubert Humphrey talks so fast that listening to him is like trying to read *Playboy* magazine with your wife turning over the pages."
Barry Goldwater, US Republican senator (1909-98)

"When I gave my big speech in the (House of) Lords, the longest letter I received was from a lady who wanted to know where I had bought my blouse."
Baroness Margaret Jay (1940-) Labour Leader of the House of Lords

"Political language ... is designed to make lies sound truthful and murder respectable, and to give an appearance of solidity to pure wind."
George Orwell

There are exceptions. The usually acerbic H L Mencken said Abraham Lincoln's Gettysburg address was the shortest and the most famous oration in American history, adding:
"It is eloquence brought to a pellucid and almost gem-like perfection – the highest emotion reduced to a few poetical phrases. Nothing else precisely like it is to be found in the whole range of oratory."

But Mencken knew a political speech when he heard one ... like that of Republican Senator Henry Cabot Lodge chairing a party convention in 1920.
His keynote speech, "of course, was bosh, but it was bosh delivered with an air – bosh somehow dignified by the manner of its emission. The same stuff, shovelled into the atmosphere by any other statesman on the platform, would have simply driven the crowd out of the hall ..."

... and speaking of bosh, here's U.S. Defence Secretary Donald Rumsfeld explaining everything and the situation in Iraq after the 2003 invasion:
"There are known knowns; there are things we know we know. We also know there are known unknowns; that is to say we know there are some things we do not know. But there are also unknown unknowns – the ones we don't know we don't know. And if one looks throughout the history of our country and other free countries, it is the latter category that tend to be the difficult ones."

NO WORRIES RUMSFELD - WE'VE RE-DEFINED TORTURE...

IRAQ-SPEAK

U.S. Defence Secretary Donald Rumsfeld was an expert at the new language Brockie dubbed Iraq Speak. Explaining the situation on the ground after the 2003 invasion of Iraq, he said: "There are known knowns; there are things we know we know. We also know there are known unknowns; that is to say we know there are some things we do not know. But there are also unknown unknowns – the ones we don't know we don't know. And if one looks throughout the history of our country and other free countries, it is the latter category that tend to be the difficult ones."

H L Mencken said of election campaigns that "a discourse packed with valid ideas, accurately expressed, is quite incomprehensible" to voters. Brockie's campaign catwalk for New Zealand's 2002 election reflected what Mencken called the "whooping of political and ecclesiastical rabble-rousers".

Campaigning

"A discourse packed with valid ideas, accurately expressed, is quite incomprehensible to (voters). What they want is the sough of vague and comforting words – words cast into phrases made familiar to them by the whooping of their customary political and ecclesiastical rabble-rousers and by the highfalutin style of the newspapers that they read."
H L Mencken

... who also observed:
"There are some politicians who, if their constituents were cannibals, would promise them missionaries for dinner."

"Anyone who says he likes it is sick."
Morris Udall, US presidential candidate (1976), sums up campaigning.

"A six-Kleenex, 40-goose-bumper, shot in the warm, golden tones of a cereal commercial."
US media magnate Ted Turner on President Ronald Reagan's 1984 campaign film for re-election.

"He is now 70. If he could provide evidence of his potency in his electoral address, he'd sweep the country."
Benjamin Disraeli, when urged to use rival Lord Palmerston's rumoured illicit love affair against him in an election campaign.

"You don't win campaigns with a diet of dishwater and milk toast."
Richard Nixon

"During an election campaign the air is full of speeches and vice versa."
Henry Adams, US historian (1838-1918)

TV has regrettably reduced the number of election meetings and therefore the time-honoured tradition of

Heckling

New Zealand Prime Minister David Lange – a recognised master of the one-liner – said he decided politics was for him at the age of eight or nine when his father took him to an election meeting where a candidate, called Gotz, angrily responded to criticism of his foreign name. Gotz said his full name was Frank Leon Albert Gotz and his initials stood for the flag. "Yeah mate, and like all flags you're up the pole!" yelled a heckler.

But Lange will always be remembered for his response to an interjector at an Oxford Union debate on nuclear weapons:
"Hold your breath just for a moment. I can smell the uranium on it."

To a woman shouting, "I wouldn't vote for you if you were the Archangel Gabriel!" Australian Prime Minister Sir Robert Menzies (1894–1978) replied:

"If I were the Archangel Gabriel, madam, I'm afraid you would not be in my constituency."

... and to a heckler who shouted: "Wotcha gonna do about 'ousing?" Sir Robert replied:
"Put an 'h' in front of it."

New Zealand Prime Minister Sir Keith Holyoake (1904–83) told a persistent and garrulous heckler:
"I am a hop-grower and you seem to be on the other end of the trade."

To a woman who interjected persistently and cried out: "Fancy being married to you!" New Zealand Labour MP Robert Semple said: "Married to you? Madam, if you and I were alone in the Garden of Eden, I'd jump the bloody fence."

Although politicians claim to take no notice of opinion polls they follow them avidly, none more so than minor parties, depicted here by Brockie disconsolately watching leaders of New Zealand's two main parties dominate the voter popularity see-saw.

In 1999, Brockie depicted a political pray-in for Winston Peters' rising polls bubble to burst.

Opinion Polls

Traditionally, politicians do not comment on opinion polls (except when they are in their favour) though they always follow them and commission them regularly in the interests of developing vote-winning policies.

But New Zealand Prime Minister Jim Bolger did comment on election night in 1996 when he did not achieve his predicted victory:

"Bugger the polls."

Election Slogans

"In your heart, you know he's right."
Barry Goldwater, US Republican presidential candidate
1984
"In your guts, you know he's nuts."
His opponents.

"Thank God only one of them can win."
Bumper sticker during Kennedy–Nixon 1960 US presidential election campaign

"Dick is a four-letter word."
Democratic campaign slogan on Republican presidential candidate Richard Nixon 1960

"Stop Repeat Offenders — Don't Re-elect Them!"
Bumper sticker in 2004 US presidential election campaign

Voting

"Vote for the man who promises least. He'll be least disappointing."
Bernard Baruch, US financier and statesman (1870-1965)

H L Mencken, perhaps the ultimate political cynic, wrote: "Giving every man a vote has no more made them wise and free than Christianity has made them good."

An equally cynical US President Harry S Truman once said:
"When a fellow tells me he's bipartisan I know he's going to vote against me."

"I never vote *for* anyone, I always vote against."
W C Fields, US actor-comedian (1879-1946)

And if you don't exercise your democratic right, bear in mind George Jean Nathan's warning:
"Bad officials are elected by good citizens who don't vote."

"One day the Don't-Knows will get in, and then where will we be?"
Spike Milligan, British comic (1918-2003)

Famous (Political) Last Words

"I am not quitting. I am staying where I am. I am going to fight the election."
Geoffrey Palmer, New Zealand Prime Minister for 13 months in 1989-90, two days before he stepped down under pressure from his Labour Party facing an election it was doomed to lose.

"I believe it is peace for our time."
Neville Chamberlain, British Prime Minister, after returning from talks with Hitler at Munich in 1938.

"I give Castro a year. No longer."
Fulgencio Batista, former president of Cuba, in 1959.

"They couldn't hit an elephant at this dist ..."
Reported (though often denied) last words of General John Sedgwick, Union general in the American Civil War, as he peered over a parapet at the Battle of Spotsylvania in 1864.

"Everywhere we are passing to the offensive, sowing insecurity in the Communists' reputedly impregnable strongholds, smashing their units one after another."
Ngo Dinh Diem, President of South Vietnam, in October 1962 .

"Vote for the man who promises least. He'll be least disappointing," said US financier Bernard Baruch. Brockie depicted long-time New Zealand Finance Minister Bill Birch promising that always elusive economic recovery.

Diem was dubbed "The Winston Churchill of Asia" by US Vice-President Lyndon Johnson, whose Central Intelligence Agency reportedly later stage-managed the military coup that toppled him, after which he was shot dead in an armoured car while leaving the country on an American guarantee of safe conduct.

When Johnson succeeded the assassinated President John F. Kennedy in 1963, he said, "I'm not going to lose Vietnam. I am not going to be the President who saw South-East Asia go the way China went."

Diem was succeeded by Major Nguyen Khanh, who was hailed by US Secretary of State Dean Rusk with the words, "Major Khanh is on the right track ... we've stabilised," two days before he was ousted in another coup.

Rusk also said in 1965:
"There is little evidence that the Viet Cong have any significant following in South Vietnam."

"I have no reason to conclude that Mr Philby has at any time betrayed the interests of this country," said British Prime Minister Harold Macmillan expressing confidence in H A R (Kim) Philby, Communist double-agent, diplomat and journalist in 1957. Philby defected to the Soviet Union in 1963.

"Iran is an island of stability in one of the more troubled areas of the world. This is a great tribute to you, Your Majesty, and to your leadership and the respect, admiration and love which your people give to you."
U.S. President Jimmy Carter to the Shah of Iran in 1977, two years before he was ousted by Ayotollah Khomeini's Islamic Revolution, which saw US diplomats in Tehran taken hostage, provoking Carter's loss to Ronald Reagan in 1980.

"As conqueror of the British Empire, I am prepared to die in defence of the motherland, Uganda."
Idi Amin, President of Uganda, in 1979, shortly before leaving for Libya to escape invading Tanzanian forces.

"No woman in my time will be Prime Minister, or Chancellor or Foreign Secretary – not the top jobs. Anyway, I wouldn't want to be Prime Minister. You have to give yourself 100 per cent."
Margaret Thatcher, October 1969, 10 years before she

Geoffrey Palmer was Prime Minister of New Zealand for just 13 months in 1989-90 before resigning under pressure from his Labour Party only 53 days before an election it was doomed to lose. Two days before he left, Palmer vowed: "I am not quitting. I am staying where I am. I am going to fight the election." Palmer's wounded head is the latest addition to Brockie's Easter Island collection of lost leaders.

became Prime Minister, going on to be Britain's longest-serving premier in the 20th century.

"Well, Mr President, you can't say that the people of Dallas haven't given you a nice welcome."
Mrs John Connally, wife of the Governor of Texas, to John F. Kennedy, as his motorcade drove through the city on November 22, 1963.

"I have often been accused of putting my foot in my mouth, but I will never put my hand in your pockets."
US Vice-President Spiro Agnew, campaigning in 1968, five years before he faced criminal charges after an investigation into tax violations.

In his resignation speech, he said:
"The intricate tangle of criminal charges levelled at me … boils down to the accusation that I permitted my fund-raising activities and my contract-dispensing activities to overlap in an unethical and an unlawful manner. Perhaps, judged by the new, post-Watergate morality, I did."

And politicians who believe they still deserve a private life should remember US President Thomas Jefferson's warning:
"When a man assumes a public trust, he should consider himself as a public property."

Henry Ward Beecher, a 19th century editor and clergyman, observed:

"Public men are bees working in a glass hive, and curious spectators enjoy themselves in watching every secret movement as if it were a study in natural history."

Index